10 IMPROVISATIONAL PIANO ETUDES
by Jeff Coffin

ISBN 9781953622105
Copyright © 2021 by Jeff Coffin. All rights reserved.
No part of this book may be duplicated or shared without the permission of Jeff Coffin.

Also available online as an e-book.
Special thanks to Josh Karas for his assistance.
Layout and cover design by Robert Hakalski.
Engraving by Kyle Gordon.
Back cover photo courtesy of Jeff Coffin.
www.jeffcoffin.com/piano

WELCOME!

What you have here are my *Ten Improvisational Piano Etudes*.

I originally played and then transcribed them on flute (also available as *10 Improvisational Flute Etudes, 10 Improvisational Clarinet Etudes, 10 Improvisational Alto Sax Etudes, 10 Improvisational Tenor Sax Etudes, 10 Improvisational Trumpet Etudes*) and they work great for piano too!

I have provided free MP3 streaming and downloads at www.jeffcoffin.com/piano so you can hear and get a feel for the solos. These etudes are performed by some of my favorite piano players: **Russell Ferrante, Howard Levy, Chris Walters, Jeff Babko, Pat Coil, and David Rodgers.**

If you want to play through them with backing tracks, which is best, I recommend getting the iRealPro app so you can change the various settings to your liking. If this is already a familiar musical language and style for you, choose your own tempo and just start playing. If not, please listen to the examples and try to imitate how the etudes are being played. I recommend taking them quite slowly at first and eventually build them up to an excruciatingly fast tempo that makes your keys smoke from the friction!! Well, I DO recommend starting slowly.

I chose the chord changes to standard jazz repertoire that I thought would be familiar, beneficial, and fun to play. I think this book has something for everyone. Oh, and I named the solos just for fun.

Some of these might be pretty challenging but it's always good to have things to work on that take some extra effort. I wouldn't want you to be bored.

The recorded tempos are for example only so it doesn't matter if you play them slower to faster than the recording when you're playing them on your own. Find tempos that work for you and that allow you to sound good and execute the material.

I hope you have a fun time with these and that you learn some things along the way. I know I did. Good luck!

Peace, JC

jeff@jeffcoffin.com
www.jeffcoffin.com/piano

TABLE OF CONTENTS

4-6 **Olive Mi** = All of Me
7 **Space Flies Like Star Pies** = Star Eyes
8-11 **Bluetude** = Blues (B♭ & C concert)
12-13 **It's The Little Things** = All The Things You Are
14-15 **Mrs. Kowalski** = Stella By Starlight
16-17 **The Answer Is Yes!** = Confirmation
18-20 **The Jones Tones** = Have You Met Miss Jones
22-23 **It's Only You** = There Will Never Be Another You
24-25 **King Of Leaps** = Giant Steps
26-27 **Where My Photos At?** = Someday My Prince Will Come

Jeff shares a treasure trove of fun and engaging material with aspiring jazz musicians of all levels. Guaranteed to expand your improvisational vocabulary!
Russell Ferrante/Piano
The Yellowjackets, Assoc. Prof. University of Southern California, multi Grammy winner,
Wayne Shorter, Joni Mitchell

•••

I had lots of fun playing Jeff's solos on piano. They are melodic, full of ideas that develop and flow. Playing these cool solos while comping is fun, a good challenge, and will help you grow as a jazz pianist.
Howard Levy/Piano
Bela Fleck & the Flecktones, multi Grammy winner, Paul Simon, Donald Fagen

•••

Jeff Coffin has spent a career and lifetime proving he can share the joy and love of music with students & listeners of all ages & skill levels. Through his etudes he now has given musicians fun new ways of getting around on their instruments, as well as being great reading exercises! It certainly won't seem like work. Jeff never "phones it in", he always gives 100% of his spirit, musicianship & experience with those in his presence.
Jeff Babko/Piano
Jimmy Kimmel Live! Band, Sheryl Crow, James Taylor, Julio Iglesias, Jason Mraz,
The B'z, Robben Ford, etc…

•••

This is a great book for any player interested in jazz and improvisation. Playing these etudes will give the student a glimpse into how to navigate these familiar chord changes in ways they might not have thought of. For myself, as a pianist, it was interesting to see how a non-piano player thinks, and specifically how Jeff Coffin thinks, which is a very good thing!
Pat Coil/Piano
Michael McDonald, Former Prof. University of North Texas, Carmen McRae,
Vince Gill, Larry Carlton

•••

Etude, Brute?
Chris Walters/Piano
JD Souther, Alabama, Bela Fleck, JC & the Mu'tet, Peter Mayer, Nashville Session Musician

•••

Jeff has created a book unlike any other, based on decades of real-world experience listening to and playing with some of the greatest jazz musicians on the planet. It's rare to find an educational resource that balances accessibility so well with creativity and immediate application - bravo, JC!
David Rodgers/Piano
Keb Mo, Taj Mahal

OLIVE MI
All of Me

Comp. **Jeff Coffin**

OLIVE MI

OLIVE MI

SPACE FLIES LIKE STAR PIES
Star Eyes

Comp. **Jeff Coffin**

BLUETUDE
Blues in B♭

Comp. **Jeff Coffin**

BLUETUDE in B♭

BLUETUDE
Blues in C

Comp. **Jeff Coffin**

BLUETUDE in C

IT'S THE LITTLE THINGS
All The Things You Are

Comp. **Jeff Coffin**

IT'S THE LITTLE THINGS

rubato - easy... fine

MRS. KOWALSKI
Stella By Starlight

Comp. **Jeff Coffin**

MRS. KOWALSKI

THE ANSWER IS YES!
Confirmation

Comp. **Jeff Coffin**

THE ANSWER IS YES!

THE JONES TONES
Have You Met Miss Jones

Comp. **Jeff Coffin**

THE JONES TONES

THE JONES TONES

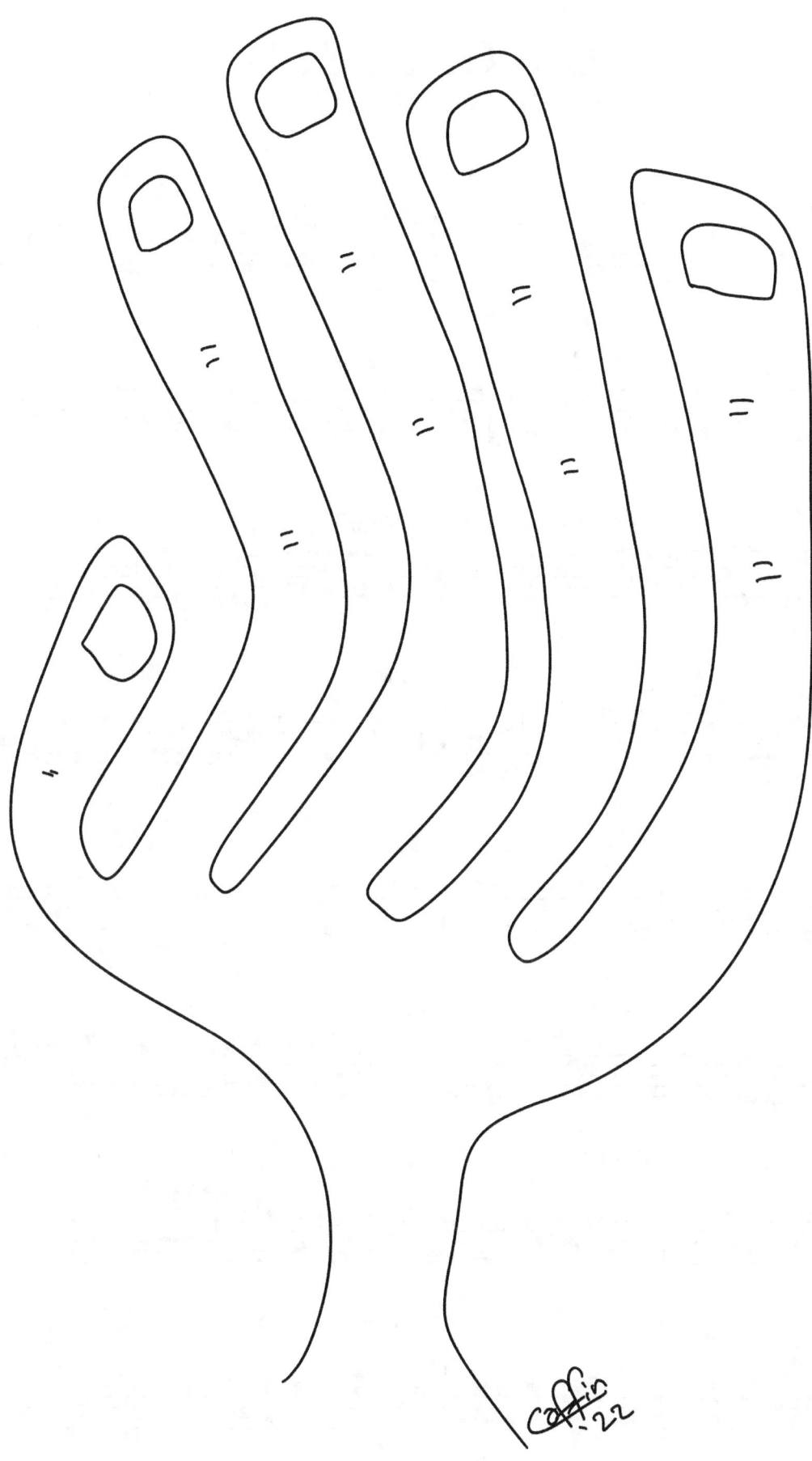

IT'S ONLY YOU
There Will Never Be Another You

Comp. **Jeff Coffin**

IT'S ONLY YOU

KING OF LEAPS
Giant Steps

Comp. **Jeff Coffin**

-24-

KING OF LEAPS

WHERE MY PHOTOS AT?
Someday My Prince Will Come

Comp. **Jeff Coffin**

-26-

WHERE MY PHOTOS AT?

ALSO BY JEFF COFFIN

10 Improvisational Flute Etudes
10 Improvisational Clarinet Etudes
10 Improvisational Alto Sax Etudes
10 Improvisational Tenor Sax Etudes
10 Improvisational Trumpet Etudes
The Road Book
The Saxophone Book (1-3)
Jeff Coffin & the Mu'tet Play-Along
The Articulate Jazz Musician (w/Caleb Chapman)

Available at **www.jeffcoffin.com**